This Coloring Book Belongs to:

____

YOU
CAN'T FIX
CRAZY.
All you can do is
DOCUMENT
IT.

WAKE UP.
KICK ASS.
Repeat.

I SEE YOU HAVE
A SEVERE CASE
OF
fucking
PRETENDINITIS

WHOEVER
HAS MY PEN,
I WILL FIND YOU
AND I WILL
Kill You

WISHING YOU A
Speedy
Recovery
FROM YOUR IMAGINARY
illness.

"BUT, I WIPE MY
OWN ASS"
SAID NO
Patient
Ever.

I HAD FUN ONCE.
Then I
WENT TO
Nursing School.

IF YOU COULD
Stop
Shitting
THE BED
THAT WOULD BE
GREAT

Dich-
head

SHIFT CHANGE
IS MY
Fucking
FAVORITE
Time of
Day

Fuck
Off!

HAPPY
School
NURSE
Day

THEY MAY
Forget
YOUR
Fucking
NAME BUT THEY
WILL NEVER
FORGET YOU

LOVE YOUR
Fucking
NURSE LIFE

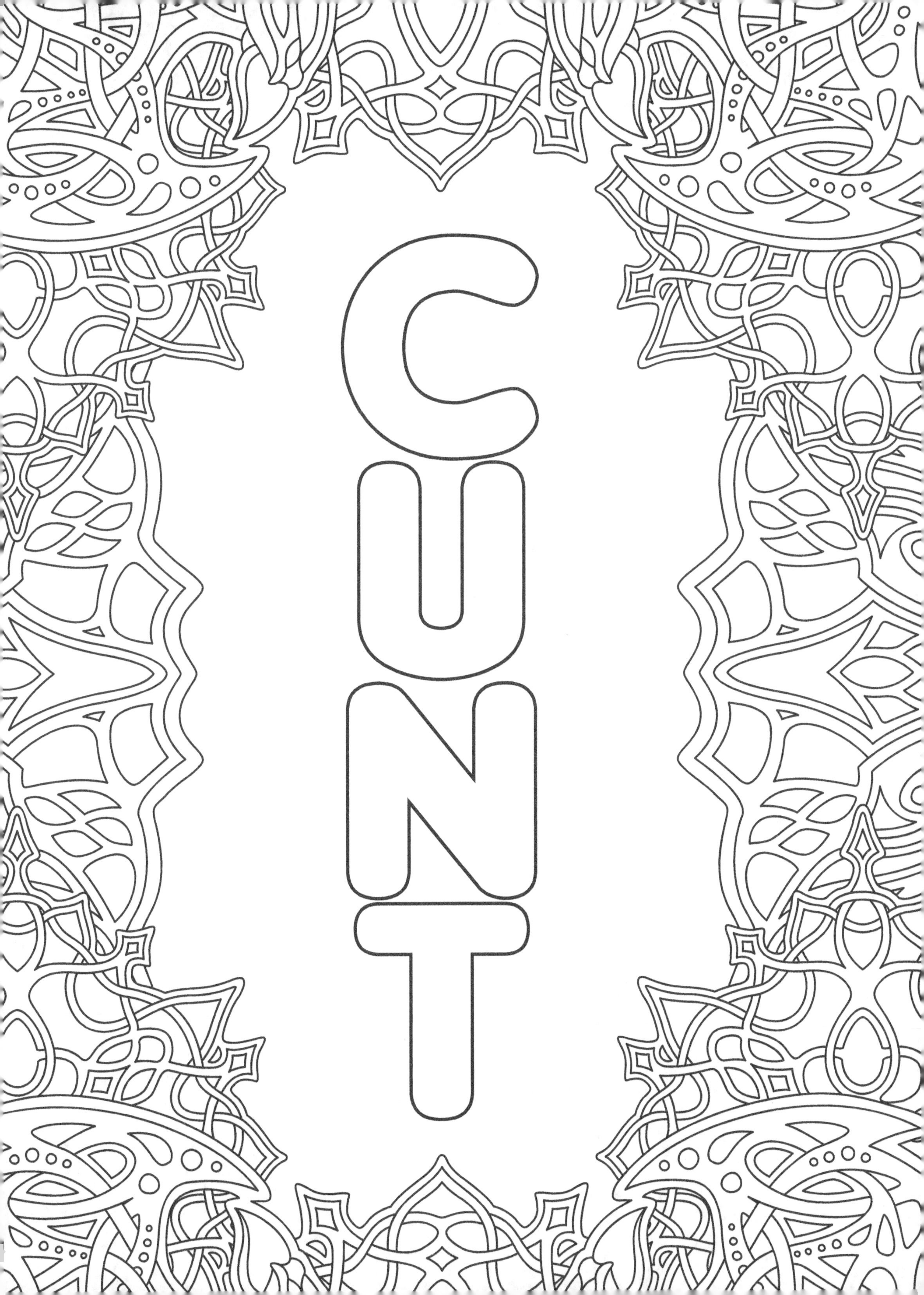
CUNT

Fuck
this
Shit

YOU CAN SCRATCH YOUR OWN DAMN NOSE

Cluster
Fuck

SON
OF A
SHIT!

KINDLY
FUCK
YOURSELF

MOI
ST

SON
OF A
MONKEY!

I'D BE A
SKINNY
NURSE

LET ME THINK... NOPE, STILL DON'T GIVE A DAMN.

HOW DID
WORK
GO?
TAKE A
FUCKING
GUESS

I'm a
Fucking
Nurse

SORRY
BOYS
I AM
COLORING

I KNOW
I SWEAR
A LOT

Make
Shit
Happens

I'm Not
a Polite
Nurse

I RUN ON
COFFEE
CHAOS &
SWEAR
WORDS

www.ingramcontent.com/pod-product-compliance
Lightning Source LLC
Chambersburg PA
CBHW080623220526
45466CB00010B/3442